purchas

Child and Youth Ministry
of St. Anne's Parish

January 2004

Meg Kimble

Shout for Joy and Sing!

For Nick

Text copyright © 2003 by Christopher L. Webber
Illustrations copyright © 2003 by Preston McDaniels

Morehouse Publishing
4775 Linglestown Road
Harrisburg, Pennsylvania 17112
www.morehousepublishing.com

Morehouse Publishing is a Continuum imprint.

Design by Tom Castanzo

A catalog record of this book is available from the Library of Congress.

ISBN 0-8192-1934-7

Printed in Malaysia
03 04 05 06 07 08   6 5 4 3 2 1

Shout for Joy and Sing!

Psalm 65 for Children

Retold by
Christopher L. Webber

Illustrated by
Preston McDaniels

MOREHOUSE PUBLISHING
A Continuum imprint
HARRISBURG · LONDON · NEW YORK

We will praise you, O God, in Jerusalem;
we will keep our promises to you
because you hear our prayers.

The things we do wrong make us sad,
but you will help us do better.

How happy are the people you invite,
who want to come to your house
and who hope to live there!
They will be happy because of the beauty of your house
and the holiness of your home.

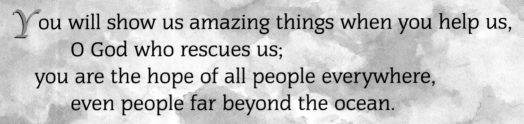

You will show us amazing things when you help us,
    O God who rescues us;
  you are the hope of all people everywhere,
    even people far beyond the ocean.

You make the mountains stand up tall by your strength;
it is your power that makes the mountains so strong.

You quiet the roaring of the ocean's waves,
the noise they make in breaking on the shore;
you calm us down as well.

$\mathcal{P}$eople all around the world will shiver with surprise
       at the wonderful things you do;
   you make the sun rise and set,
       and you make the morning and evening sing for joy.

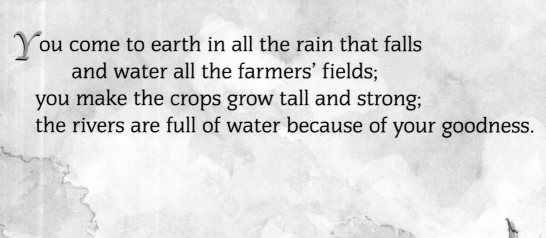

You come to earth in all the rain that falls
    and water all the farmers' fields;
you make the crops grow tall and strong;
the rivers are full of water because of your goodness.

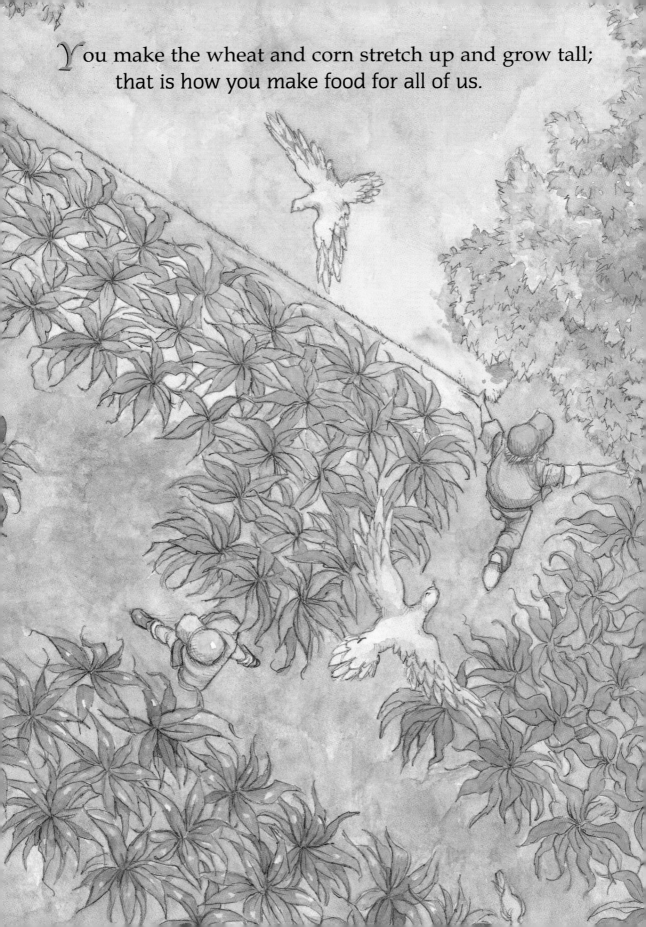

You make the wheat and corn stretch up and grow tall;
that is how you make food for all of us.

You water the ridges that are left behind the plow
and smooth out the soil with your showers of rain;
you soften the ground with heavy rain
and bless the growing plants.

Every year is wonderful because of your goodness,
      and everywhere you go
      there is more than enough for all.

Lord, grant that even the poorest fields
       may have thick grass for the cattle to eat;
let even the grass on the hills
       be glad to serve your purpose.

Let the meadows be covered with flocks of sheep,
and let grain fill the valleys like a flood;
let hills and valleys shout for joy and sing.

Christopher L. Webber is the author of over a dozen books, and his hymns appear in several major hymnals. He has ministered to inner-city, suburban, and overseas parishes, and he currently serves two small congregations in rural northwestern Connecticut. He has been married for over 40 years to Margaret Elisabeth Webber; they have four grown children and three grandchildren.

Photo by Hal Maggiore

Preston McDaniels' interest in art began as a young child when he entertained himself by drawing. He also fell in love with music as a child, and still plays his trusty piano each morning. He combined his love of music and his talent for illustration in four critically acclaimed books of hymns for children, *God of the Sparrow, All Things Bright and Beautiful*, *Earth & All Stars*, and *Now the Day Is Over*, all available from Morehouse Publishing. He lives in Nebraska with his wife, Cindy, and two daughters, Abby and Lizzie.